Healing Soul Misery:
Finding the Pathway Home

Susan Gleeson

Published by Lulu.com

ISBN: 978-0-557-74685-9

For David and for Doug,

Who each asked for a "handbook"
and thus gave me the idea.

Thank you both so much!

TABLE OF CONTENTS

Acknowledgments

In my life I have twenty "believing mirrors" -- fellow artists/ writers/ dancers/ life coaches/beloved family members and friends who are each seeking to live out their compelling purpose for being here on this planet. These people are my most treasured fellow sojourners. They see me clearly, and they have encouraged me unstintingly as I have written this book.

"Friendship is a strong and habitual inclination in two persons to promote the good and happiness in one another." Eustace Budgell

I have found such friends, and I will be forever grateful for them!

I have discovered that it not only takes a village to raise a child, it takes a village to write and publish a book. Thank you so much Joan Williams, my "word-smith" editor, and Nick Kettles, my "big-picture" editor, for your diligence, patience and brilliance. Thank you to Sheri Burnham for creating the graphic design for this second book and thank you for helping me navigate Lulu. For all the laughter along the way, I am truly grateful. You made things easy!

Introduction: Defining Soul Misery

A good-looking young businessman sat across from me in my coaching room and began to speak. "I have a lovely wife, two healthy children, a challenging job, a beautiful home and an expensive car. I have no reason to feel this way, yet every day, I feel like driving my car into a tree."

In the past eight years of being a life coach, I have worked with many such individuals. I have also met them during the course of my day-to-day medical practice -- people who seem to "have it made", yet despite having it all, feel an inner desperation.

I call this situation Soul Misery because the condition of apparently having it all, yet feeling empty and rudderless, produces a state of extreme suffering. This suffering is felt in a place within us that is somehow different than the mind or the heart. This suffering is felt deep within the core of ourselves, within that place we call our soul.

As I observed and studied Soul Misery, I asked some sufferers to try to define it for me, and to try to articulate some of the experience of their suffering.

Some experience Soul Misery as not knowing who they are.

"It's a state of desperation, without much hope for change to occur. It is confusion. It is a yearning to discover where the pain is really coming from. It's feeling like giving up. The world has no color. There's emotion, but no passion. There's existence, but no sense of light. Every once in a while, however, there is a spark -- enough to keep seeking."

Some sufferers report a sense of who they are, but do not feel the freedom to express that authentic self.

"It's a deep, melancholic longing to simply be accepted for who I am, for my unique voice to be heard."

"It's feeling that I have to be someone other than I am to survive in this world, to please others. It's a form of prostitution or bondage. It is believing that when I get somewhere other than here, I will be enough or have enough."

"It's like being in a strait jacket, or having a pillow over my face. My soul is simply suffocating with restraint."

For others, the misery seems born of not knowing why they are here.

"It's about feeling disconnected and isolated. It's never feeling authentic, doing what others want you to do, and not even knowing what YOU want to do."

The experience of Soul Misery also involves fear of rejection.

"If I really let you see who I am, will you still want to be with me?" I continually morph myself into what I think you might want me to be."

Others again describe Soul Misery as the pain of not being seen for who they are.

"It's the dark chill of never being seen."

"It's the relentless, crushing darkness and gnawing pain of loneliness."

"It's the experience of having little or nothing reflected back to me of my true nature. Hell might be another term for it."

Soul Misery probably sounds like depression to many people, yet it is not depression, although Soul Misery -- if allowed to go on too long -- can slip into a depression that co-exists with this condition.

Depression has classic symptoms and signs, such as difficulty with sleep, a lack of interest in life, strong feelings of guilt where it is not warranted, decreased energy, poor concentration, alterations of appetite, and decreased sexual interest. I have seen many people with Soul Misery who had none of these symptoms and signs, and who, in fact, were highly functioning members of society. Soul misery is a more existential experience because the person is searching deeply for the meaning in their life; they desperately need to know what it is. It regards knowing clearly who they are and why they are here, as well as having someone else see it, too.

Soul Misery is not grief. There is no loss of a loved one involved. Rather, it is a state of "not knowing", accompanied by an equally strong inner conviction that there must be something more. It is a feeling of not really knowing oneself, as well as not knowing why one is on the planet. And in that state of confusion, of not knowing, is the exquisite pain of being aware that no one else can see clearly "who I am". There is neither the sense of deep contentment in the belly that arises from really knowing oneself, nor the deep joy of being truly seen by another.

Soul Misery is suffering that exists in the core of one's very Self, the most secret and private and important part of one's being. The misery is the pain of knowing that there is more to one's life, to the essence of oneself, than one has seen, or known, or been consciously aware of before. It is also the sense that this essence could be, and should be, able to be known, but one doesn't yet have the map or the key to the knowing. And the misery comes from being desperate to unfold that map and hold that key.

Sound familiar?

This may seem a grim and a dark situation, yet the good news is that Soul Misery can be alleviated. There is a way to find the pathway home to yourself.

When you come to know yourself, your gifts, talents and abilities, your purpose for being on this planet at this time in history, your Soul Misery will begin to lift. It is relieved even more when you start to live out your purpose on the planet, using all of your gifts, talents and abilities.

And when at least one other person can see you clearly -- "get you", accept you in a non-judgmental fashion, find you interesting, and become your friend -- Soul Misery can be healed.

In this book, my intention is to make this path plain enough for you, or for a loved one of yours, to follow. Deciding to embark on this path takes curiosity, courage, honesty, patience and endurance. It helps tremendously to have an older and wiser journeying partner like your family doctor, a life coach, a counselor or a spiritual adviser to accompany you because they can often show you the next step to take in your process of healing.

You wouldn't be reading this book unless you had a feeling that you, too, may be suffering from Soul Misery, or that you may know someone who is. You are in no way alone in having this experience in the world. Come with me, and we will begin the process of knowing yourself, knowing your gifts, talents and abilities, and getting a sense of the unique purpose for which you were created.

CHAPTER 1: MY STORY

When I went into medicine, I was sure I would be seeing patients who -- under my care -- would get better and better, and need me less and less. This, sadly, did not turn out to be the case.

After twenty years practicing as a family physician, I was feeling more and more discouraged. I was devoted to my patients, sharing all my knowledge and skill with them, yet often they were not cured of their chronic conditions -- problems such as depression, anxiety, obsessive-compulsive disorder, fibromyalgia, addiction, morbid obesity, career misfit and marriage problems.

Moreover, I had the distinct feeling that many of my patients didn't need to suffer; somehow, somewhere, there existed an answer or a cure. However, I didn't know what that was.

I read books, attended courses and seminars. I applied a few tips that helped some patients. I prayed with my patients and talked with them about spiritual answers to their problems. Some were helped, yet far too many still were left struggling with their problems.

I even spoke with my mentor, an older and wiser family physician, about my frustration. He told me that, sadly, medicine could not be expected to cure people, and that we practice medicine mostly to ease our patients' pain and suffering, not to cure it. For me, hearing these words was heart-rending.

I began to go for long walks of despair. I walked around my neighborhood every evening, crying out to God and asking him why, if I were a physician, meaning "one who heals", why could I not find out how to heal my patients at the deepest level.

I felt sad, alone and a little ridiculous for feeling what others didn't seem to feel. I tried to be content with doing good each day for my patients, but this didn't satisfy me. Not being able to heal deeply began to seem like it was devouring my own soul. Feeling like a misfit in my chosen profession, I began thinking about giving up my work. But I didn't know what I wanted to do instead. I felt "stuck". My situation began to feel more and more untenable.

I didn't realize it at the time, but this terrible feeling of being "stuck" was the very thing that many of my patients were experiencing. It was no wonder I felt so frustrated and upset each day at work; I was essentially looking at myself and my own struggles in the lives of many of the patients I was trying to treat. We were all feeling miserable, stuck and alone, together.

One lovely spring evening, I was on one of my walks, enjoying the smell of the damp, fresh earth. Without warning, a strange thing happened. In my mind's eye, in the upper corner of my left visual field, I saw the image of a purple crocus. I thought, Oh no! Not only do I feel hopelessly stuck, and confused and frustrated, I'm also going crazy. I didn't think it was a hallucination, but if it weren't that, what was it? I had certainly never heard of anything similar happening to anyone else.

Although this image remained constantly in my mind's eye for the next few months, I could not think of anyone I could confide in about its presence. It was just too strange an experience. I still felt miserable, yet I felt a flicker of hope that something was about to happen, something that could bring insight and help.

One day, an article in the local newspaper profiled a new person starting a business in our community, a "life coach". In the article, the coach said that when people felt stuck in their lives, she could help them change things that were holding them back. Because I was feeling so stuck and did not know whom to consult, this article gave me hope. I contacted the life coach and asked if she would be willing to meet with me. She agreed. I liked her kindness -- her confidence and calmness, so I took a chance and told her about the crocus in my mind's eye. I asked her what it might mean. She just smiled, advised me to get a picture of a crocus to put on my desk, look at it, and see what happened next.

I did this, and to my pleasure and relief, the image of the crocus disappeared from my mind's eye. I looked at the picture of the crocus and realized that for me as a gardener, crocuses herald spring, new life, the end of winter and hope. I began to believe that the image might have been given to me to herald a new season in my own life. I realized that if the life coach had been able to provide me with this insight, then maybe I should look into receiving some life coaching, and even consider becoming a life coach myself. I studied the website of the Coaches Training Institute, and liking what I saw, signed up for the first course toward becoming a life coach.

I was so excited and impatient for the course date to arrive; yet when it did, I entered the conference room feeling ill at ease. There were no other physicians present. As we began, I felt awkward. Concepts such as values, fulfillment, balance and perspectives were introduced to me, concepts with which I was completely unfamiliar. I felt like a fish out of water, definitely.

That night, staying on my own in the hotel, I developed a migraine. The next morning I did not want to return for another day. Yet, I felt desperate for relief from my sense of being stuck and from my despair, so I forced myself to go back into the conference room.

The leaders called for a volunteer to come forward to be coached so they could demonstrate to the other participants how life coaching occurred in real time. Although I was feeling sick and miserable, one thing was clear: I was in desperate need of life coaching. So I put up my hand and was selected immediately. I tentatively went forward and sat opposite the coach in the chair that had been set up at the front of the room. As I looked at her she looked back with kind, blue eyes. She seemed confident and at ease with herself, wise and knowledgeable. I felt I could trust her.

The coach began by asking me a question she says she had never asked before and has never asked since: What color is your life?

I began to sob uncontrollably and choked out the answer. "Gray."

"And what color do you want it to be?"

A voice emerged from deep inside me. "Spring green."

She asked, who took your spring green? And we were off.... As she continued to ask me a series of powerful questions -- very useful questions, unlike any I had ever been asked before -- I felt the doors of self-knowledge begin to open. By the end of the half hour my migraine was gone, and I had a feeling of having gone from death to life.

I did not feel horribly stuck anymore. Above all, I had the feeling there was hope for me... hope to find my way in my profession, hope to be able to be a more effective healer of my patients, hope to be able to understand myself and the meaning of my own life.

I actually skipped around the room I was feeling so much better. It was difficult to sit down and concentrate for the rest of the weekend. I signed up for the remainder of the coaching courses, reasoning that if I felt this much better from one half-hour coaching session, then learning more would be wonderful for me personally and for the patients under my care.

I felt like I had been given a new set of tools to use in my work. They were novel to me, practical, fresh and fun, and I could hardly wait to try them on my patients in the office.

The first day home, I couldn't stop talking about my experience to my husband, my children and my friends. I don't think I made much sense to them, but in my excitement and joy, they clearly could see that something had changed dramatically for me, and for the better.

When the Grass Looks Greener

The next morning I went for a walk. This walk was so different from the strolls I had previously been taking in my neighborhood. It was all I could do to keep from skipping. The grass looked greener, the sky was bluer and everything in my world seemed more wonderful.

I was passing a friend's house and felt a strong urge to go in to see him. I went, and told him how terrible I had been feeling, and how wonderful I was feeling now. I couldn't contain my joy and talked on and on about my experiences.

Suddenly, my quiet, shy, reserved, intense friend burst into tears. He cried out, "You are my angel! I have been waiting for you to come. I feel so miserable and I want you to be my life coach."

I was flabbergasted. "No," I stuttered. "I don't think I can do it. I've only had three days of training so far. But I will definitely help you to find an experienced life coach."

He said emphatically, "NO! I want you."

So, I agreed to try to help him and we set a time to meet. With great excitement, and at the same time great trepidation, I rushed home to email one of the lead coaches. "Guess what? I have my first client. Now what do I do?"

That afternoon, I went to the office. About sixteen patients had scheduled appointments. Still feeling the powerful effect of the weekend coaching questions, I decided to ask them of my patients: What color is your life? What color do you want it to be?

One of my drug-addicted patients came in. He was an intimidating man and I was a little frightened to query him. Yet, when I asked what color he wanted his life to be, he immediately replied, "Sky blue."

As I asked him more about "sky blue", he recounted the one day in his life that he knew his father loved him. His dad had taken him out for a day of fishing, and the sky was a beautiful blue and the water reflected that color, too. His dad and he enjoyed a perfect day together.

As he talked about this experience, something within me shifted. I found I could access love for my patient for the first time, instead of my previous attitude of judgment and fear. The same thing seemed to happen within him and we both started crying. We talked for a while longer, and we both realized that something had altered profoundly within us and within our relationship. After that day, I never again feared him or saw him as a nuisance. He became a person for me, another suffering person, whom I could see and know better. Our doctor-patient relationship improved profoundly.

As I gained experience in life coaching, I saw that many of my patients did not have a clear idea of their direction in life. They were confused, dissatisfied and restless, just like I was. Often my patients reported that they experienced their pain internally, while in the outside world, they carried out their duties and responsibilities in a normal fashion. No one could tell that anything was wrong, or that they were experiencing such deep internal pain.

I came to realize that the condition I was suffering from, as well as my neighbour and my drug-addicted patient and untold others, was what I have come to call Soul Misery.

Over my eight years of being a life coach, I have treated approximately one hundred people with this condition. Although there is no one-size-fits-all definition of soul misery, what is common to all sufferers is an inability to see, experience, or express clearly -- either to themselves or others -- their true and authentic selves.

This *seeing of self* takes time, and seems to come in stages.

For instance, I thought that discovering life coaching would heal my own soul misery completely, and indeed, it seemed to for a period of time. However, after a short while, feelings of restlessness and dissatisfaction resurfaced; I still didn't know all of myself, parts of myself were still to be discovered.

Again I saw images in my mind's eye. I got up my courage to tell an artist friend about them. With combined hope and trepidation, I told her I thought I could be an artist! Without batting an eye, she asked me what kind of art and what kind of medium I was drawn to. I even had to ask what kind of mediums there were.

My friend asked me to find a painting that would illustrate the kind of art I wanted to make. I told her about a painting in a downtown store window. She went to see the piece and was able to tell me that it was an abstract acrylic painting.

I blurted out, "Could you help me begin to make acrylic abstracts?"

She smiled. "Of course."

My friend was soon guiding me along the aisles of an art supply store. We bought a huge canvas, some acrylic paints, an easel and some brushes. The next day my friend came to my home and helped me clear a space in the spare bedroom and put up my easel. I began. I simply chose colors that I liked and applied paint to the canvas. My friend patiently and quietly stood by and supported me as I painted, mixing colors that I wanted, but didn't have.

As I began to paint, strong feelings overcame me. I laughed, I cried, I shouted. I felt angry. In each of these states I kept painting on my huge 36 x 36 inch canvas. I kept going for six hours, until finally my husband poked his head into the room, telling me it was way past dinner hour.

It was as though a dam inside me had broken and the unrecognized artist inside me had been released. The relief! I felt I'd discovered -- and recovered -- a piece of myself. This led, again, to a feeling of pure joy, the very opposite of the Soul Misery "grayness" that I had been feeling for years.

I completed about fifty paintings in the next year. The romantic notion that ideas and images could be locked up inside of someone, longing to be expressed, proved true. I found a nearby community college artist offering a week-long Introduction to Acrylic Abstract course. I signed up, and had a wonderful time learning some of the principles of painting these abstracts.

Over time, I learned to recognize a pattern within myself. Restlessness and a feeling of misery signaled the need to discover, explore and express another hidden piece of me. I went through this cycle many times in the years ahead as I explored my own Soul Misery and sought to heal it.

A quotation attributed to Sri Ramakrishnan says, *"Do not seek illumination unless you seek it as a man whose hair is on fire seeks a pond."* (Campbell 25) Indeed, most Soul Misery sufferers I have coached come to me because they have reached the point in their lives where the pain is so great they are willing to do whatever it takes to relieve that misery. Their subsequent journey turns out to be one of discovery and an increasing sense of relief as slowly, but surely, these individuals recover the parts of themselves that have been lost.

In order to begin the journey of discovery, it is necessary to consider the cause of Soul Misery. I have discovered that there are three key components that combine to create this situation. In the next chapter we will explore each component in detail. Let's begin!

Chapter 2: Reasons for Soul Misery

Domestication

A lovely young university graduate came into my office to see me for some life coaching.

She said, "I *know* I'm smart, and I *know* that there's something that I am born to do here on earth, but I don't know what it is. I went to the university student health services counselor to ask for help, but we didn't really connect. She didn't understand what I was asking for, and she didn't "see" me clearly. I was prescribed an antidepressant by the student health doctor, and I feel a little better, but I don't know what to do next with my life. I don't know for sure what I'm good at. Sometimes I feel happy, but sometimes I just despair of ever finding my place or my way to contribute, and I sob for hours on my bed. Can you help me find out who I am, and what I am really good at?"

How does it happen that intelligent and gifted people can complete university degrees, yet still have these questions about themselves? Like this young woman, most people I begin to coach have a deep sense that there is a purpose for them -- a reason to be here -- yet they can't connect with it. Although it makes sense that it is important to have a clear idea of who we are and why we are here, in our day and age, in North American Society, the belief that people have a unique purpose seems to be unusual. This idea isn't talked about in our homes; neither is it a task that is prioritized. Thus, when someone expresses unhappiness about not knowing who they are, health care professionals may misinterpret it as evidence of depression, especially if the person displays some of the clinical signs and symptoms of depression.

Rather than focusing on helping children discover who they are and why they are here, children go through a process of what writer Don Miguel Ruiz terms "domestication." In his book, <u>The Four Agreements</u>, Ruiz says when we are born, we become subject to what he terms *the dream of the planet.*

"The dream of the planet includes all of society's rules, its beliefs, its laws, its religions, its different cultures, and ways to be, its governments, schools, social events, and holidays. We are born

with the capacity to learn how to dream, and the humans who live before us teach us how to dream the way society dreams. The outside dream has so many rules that when a new human is born, we hook the child's attention and introduce these rules into his or her mind. The outside dream uses Mom and Dad, the schools and religions to teach us how to dream." (Ruiz 2-3)

In other words, in North American society, parents usually socialize a newborn child according to the rules of society, rather than focusing on the uniqueness of their child, trying to draw out and encourage that uniqueness. They seek to mold and shape a child to be a good citizen within the family and the society in which he/she lives, rather than focusing on looking deeply for the inherent gifts, talents and abilities of that child to surface (his/her original design), and then molding and shaping those attributes. Teachers, ministers, aunts and uncles tend to focus on the child in the same way.

We humans need the attention of our parents and relatives, and we learn that we can get it if we fall into line with what they think and believe, and act in a way that pleases them.

We soon learn that we may be dismissed or punished for behavior that does not correspond with the values of these significant adults in our lives.

Our need for approval is strong. In fact, as children we tend to equate our parents' approval with our parents' love; we desperately need both, because we need our parents to survive. If it becomes a choice between following our natural inclinations or winning our parents' love and approval, we will, for survival, do whatever it takes to achieve the latter.

This behavior is inherited, passed down from one generation to the next. Our caregivers were socialized in the exact same manner, and their parents before them. Who knows where the belief originated that all people should be socialized in the same manner? We say, of course, that each child is an individual and should be regarded and reared as such, yet this is not what happens in most homes. Uniform training and uniform behavior may make for a more cohesive society, but at what cost?

As children we have no way of knowing that the acceptance of society and the approval of our parents is not as fulfilling as the deep contentment found in knowing ourselves and fulfilling our purpose in this world, and so we generally agree to the domestication process.

The system of reward and punishment for conforming or not conforming to the group is compelling, as well.

For instance, if by nature you are a quiet person who enjoys your own company, but are told by your parents that spending time alone in your room is bad or wrong, then you will tend to go against your natural inclination to enjoy time alone, and seek out the group. You will tend to reject your desire to do something other than what your mom or dad says, even if it is to follow your own natural inclinations. Your fear of punishment, or your desire for reward and acceptance, makes doing what you have been programmed to do feel a whole lot safer.

Likewise, a person who needs lots of time to complete a task, but is told she must progress at the same pace as the group, will suffer greatly because her internal sense of pacing is repeatedly violated.

As well, children who may be naturally inclined to make art, or dance, or playact, may be told that these activities are a waste of time, and that devoting time to science or sports is more worthy of a young person's time and attention.

It is a terrible paradox that allowing ourselves to be domesticated draws us away from experiencing our true selves, something that we desperately need. This is one of the things that make the experience of Soul Misery so distressing.

Two forces act upon us: the external draw, which pulls us in the direction of being and doing what our parents and society want (in order to find acceptance within the group), and the internal draw, the deep pull of the soul and its design, which compels us to inhabit our own unique and original design.

The pain of Soul Misery comes from being unaware of what is causing this terrible tension within us. The pain compounds when we do not know how to hear and respond to our soul's voice. We have little or no experience at recognizing or responding to its call.

Another young coaching client told me about her experience of domestication. She said she was reading an article in a magazine that used the phrase *"anorexia of the soul"*. She said the phrase reminded her of the concept of Soul Misery. She believed she could relate so well to both terms because for years she had lived in that internal place. She said that, for her, Soul Misery was a state of imprisonment, which was especially scary because although she knew she was trapped, it appeared that other people could not see or comprehend her suffering. This young woman felt deeply unfulfilled and lacked hope for her future. She had attained things others felt were important, but these things were not giving her a sense of life. And there were times when she would be surrounded by people, yet feel completely alone. She said this feeling was unbearable. When she managed to put on a mask of feeling okay, she felt fake and ashamed for what felt, to her, like living a lie. This young woman was experiencing the deep pain of knowing she was imprisoned and the profound ache of feeling she was in no way fulfilled in her life. She could not see a way to change things and she did not know clearly what was wrong.

A Good Enough Reason

There comes a day when trying to fit into other peoples' ideas of who you are and how you should behave becomes too painful. You have tried, but find no satisfaction from "fitting in" behavior. Your soul is deeply miserable, and so you decide to strike out and find your own way. The thought of going a different route and embarking on a path that runs counter to our domestication can generate intense and fearful feelings.

Taking a stand for our right to choose our own ways and beliefs requires courage. Taking the risk to try to discover who we are is unlikely to be supported by the parents, ministers and teachers who socialized us -- especially if the way we want to go is not their way. To begin healing our souls, therefore, we may even have to be willing to forgo the acceptance of our parents or peers for a period of time while we make the changes we need to make.

We have to be both miserable enough and courageous enough to take action. We also have to have some sense of what the pathway is, how to find it, and how to begin to walk upon it. It helps to know someone who has walked the path ahead of us -- someone who models another way, a way that resonates in some deep place within your soul, someone who is more like you, someone who can "see" who you really are.

This individual can give us hope that going against our domestication is a worthwhile risk to take. Stepping away from the path of domestication seems possible when we can envision the rewards. By deciding to live in line with the essence of yourself, you will begin to regain your personal power. When you do that, you regain, or experience for the first time, a sense of recognizing yourself and with that comes some ease and some peace. This is a fabulous feeling!

So, domestication is a process that all human beings go through. It assumes that all of us should be socialized in much the same way, and does not take into account the uniqueness of the individual. Because we need and crave our parents' approval, we go along with it. It is possible, then, to arrive at adulthood unaware of our unique gifts, talents and abilities. Because of this, we can end up in careers that do not suit us in any way. This situation can produce profound distress, of feeling pulled in opposite directions. We feel alone and misunderstood. Eventually these feelings can become overwhelming and intolerable.

One of the key things the domestication process does is either suppress or reinforce our unique personality type. In the next section we shall explore the relevance of personality type to both the development and the healing of Soul Misery.

PERSONALITY TYPE

As I began to work with people to discover their original design, I came across the book <u>Do What You Are</u> by Paul D. Tieger and Barbara Barron Tieger. This book taught me about the Myers Briggs personality typing system and its foundational premise: that knowing your particular personality type will give you important information to help you choose the most appropriate career for yourself.

I found this a fascinating idea, and as part of my work with clients, I began to determine each life coaching client's Myers Briggs personality type using the tool provided in the Tiegers' book.

In doing this with hundreds of people, I came to see that many people -- although they tested as a certain personality type -- were not *living* that personality type. I came to understand that Soul Misery occurs when *anyone* of *any* personality type is living a long way off their type.

Just as the domestication process is able to throw *any* or essentially *all* of us off our original design, being unaware of our personality type can do the same thing.

So, what is the Myers Briggs personality typing system and how can we be living "off type"?

Throughout history, there have been two basic ways to look at the behavior of human beings. Hippocrates thought that infants are born with their personality type and temperament already determined. Galenof Pergamon, a Roman physician, agreed with Hippocrates, and this viewpoint (that people are born with predispositions as opposed to being largely malleable) persisted until the early twentieth century. The Russian scientist Ivan Pavlov proposed something completely different. He believed that behavior was simply a "mechanical response to certain environmental stimulation." (Keirsey 2)

John Watson, the first American behaviorist, claimed that he could "shape a child into any form he wanted by conditioning, provided that the child was put in his charge while yet an infant." (Keirsey 2)

Psychiatrist Sigmund Freud and others of his day believed that people are all fundamentally alike: their behavior is driven from within by a single, basic motive. But Freud disagreed with psychologists such as Maslow, Sullivan and Adler as to what that motive was. Freud believed our single basic motive was instinctual lust. Abraham Maslow said it was based in self-actualization. Harry Sullivan said our paramount motivation was social solidarity, while Alfred Adler contended it was to achieve superiority. (Keirsey 3)

In 1920, Swiss psychiatrist Carl Jung returned to the idea that people differ from one another in essential ways. He proposed that individuals have a natural inclination toward either extraversion or introversion. He went on to say that people have preferences for certain basic psychological functions: thinking, feeling, sensation and intuition. He believed that our preference for a given function is so innate that we can be identified, or "typed", according to this preference. (Keirsey 3)

Nonetheless, psychology continued to be dominated by Freud and Pavlov's thinking until the 1940s. Then two American women, Kathryn Briggs and her daughter, Isabel Briggs Myers, read Carl Jung's 1923 book, Psychological Types. They went on to study Jung's work, build upon it and expand his findings. The mother-daughter team gave Jung's theory a practical application by developing the Myers Briggs type indicator test (MBTI), which is a detailed document designed to measure psychological type.

Jung documented three personality preferences and eight personality types; Myers and Briggs, based on their many years of study, identified four personality preferences and sixteen distinct personality types.

Instead of naming her sixteen personality types with descriptive words, Myers elected to label them with a combination of letters chosen from four pairs of alternatives, E or I, S or N, T or F, J or P. The letters represent the following words:

E= Extraverted   or   I= Introverted

S= Sensory   or   N=Intuitive

T= Thinking   or   F= Feeling

J= Judging   or   P= Perceiving

Myers described being extraverted as having an "expressive" and outgoing social attitude.

Introverted means having a "reserved" and reclusive attitude.

Sensory means being highly "observant" of things in the immediate environment.

Intuitive means being "introspective" or highly imaginative of things seen only with the mind's eye.

Thinking means being "tough minded" or objective and impersonal with others.

Feeling means being "friendly" or sympathetic and personal with others.

Judging means being given to making and keeping schedules.

Perceiving means looking around for alternatives, opportunities and options, hence probing or exploring. (Keirsey 12-13)

The MBTI caught on so well that by the 1990s, over a million people worldwide were taking the test each year. As a physician and life coach with the privilege of seeing many people over a long period of time, I came to agree deeply with Carl Jung's thesis that people differ from each other in these basic, essential ways. And as I began to "type" people, I got to observe them as they experienced moments of increased self-knowledge arising from understanding their personality type.

Living Off Type Leads to Soul Misery

For example, one client was very much an introvert (I), an intuitive (N), a feeler (F) and a perceiver (P), but because of his domestication process he was encouraged to live as an extravert (E) a sensor (S), a thinker (T) and a judger (J). He came in for coaching because of extreme Soul Misery. He was spending a lot of his time alone, just sitting and staring into space.

Jim was a quiet (I), bookish young man who was born into a family of extraverted (E) sports lovers. He wanted to stay home and read quietly by the hour (P), but his parents wanted him to play various team sports. He wanted his parents' love and approval, so he gamely joined in even though he was somewhat clumsy and uncoordinated. Jim had limited success at any team sport he tried. He was very interested in art and was considering pursuing a career as an abstract artist (N), but his parents told him briskly that this was a waste of time (T). Jim was told he would never be able to make a living being an artist, and instead, he should go to business school (SJ). This totally went against the grain, yet, to try to please his parents, Jim did attend business school. However, because he did so poorly, he was not allowed to continue.

Jim worked for a few years and saved up the money to return to university in the program of his choice. While in the Bachelor of Fine Arts program, Jim met some kindred spirits who shared his love of art, books and hours of deep conversation (F). At last, he began to feel at home in his own skin; he had the experience of "being seen". Jim went on to become a university professor, well respected by his peers.

Jim is an example of a young man who was born with a certain personality type, but because of domestication, was encouraged to live the life of a different personality type. Jim felt increasingly lost and miserable as he tried to balance the competing pulls of pleasing his parents yet following his natural inclinations. As he got older, Jim was able to find the inner strength to follow his own interests. Jim was aided in this by finding people more like he was, with whom he could feel at home and be truly seen and accepted. Jim realized he was not an "ugly duckling", but rather a swan born into a duck family!

Sometimes people are living off their personality type by only one letter -- or component -- rather than all the letters. Still, this can cause a state of Soul Misery that feels just as acute. This was Mary's story. She is an ISFJ, but was raised by parents who were both thinkers, and so she had been socialized to be an ISTJ.

Mary's family respected logic and reason (T). She had always thought her family relationships were positive, and therefore, considered the advice that she received from family members to be trustworthy. Mary knew her parents deeply cared for her and wanted her to be happy. When Mary became aware of her personality type and studied it, she realized that the way she was nurtured and guided within her family was actually keeping her from discovering and living out who she truly was. This was no fault of theirs and completely unintentional, yet the nurturing style Mary needed as an emotional/feelings (F) person was not central to the style of parenting (T) that she had received. Being an emotionally wired (F) person within a logically wired (T) world, this was a difficult situation for her to detect. However, once Mary discovered this truth, she felt a newfound freedom and excitement at the thought of exploring more deeply her personality, gifts and dreams.

Not being seen as an (F) had led Mary to feel out-of-step and miserable in a way she could not understand until she became aware of the Myers Briggs typing system and was "typed" herself. Becoming aware of who she was brought relief and freedom almost instantly. And this has been the case with many coaching clients who previously had no way of understanding why they felt so different from the people around them.

Certain Personality Types are Prone to Soul Misery

Over the past eight years of typing people, I have discovered that Soul Misery sufferers I have worked with are prone to one of three personality types. These are the INFJ, the INFP, and the ISFP personality types.

These three types are rare in the population, representing approximately two to three percent, three to four percent, and five to seven percent of the American population respectively, compared to other more common personality types, such as ESTJ, which represents twelve to fifteen percent of the population. (Barron-Tieger and Tieger 34, 37, 43, 50) Thus, the chance of people of the former personality types being reared in families who are familiar with those types is smaller, and these folks are the ones most likely to suffer from feeling like "ugly ducklings" in their families of origin.

After the publication of the Myers-Briggs Type Indicator, David Keirsey, an American psychologist, also became interested in typing people. He found it useful to partition Myer's sixteen types into four groups. Isabel Myers herself had suggested that all four of what she referred to as "NFs" were alike in many ways, as were all four of the "NTs". Keirsey noticed that the "SJs" were also very similar, as were the "SPs". He called these four groups "temperaments". In his book, Please Understand Me II, David Keirsey describes the characteristics of each of these four groups in detail.

INFJs and INFPs are part of the NF temperament called the Idealists. Of NFs, Keirsey says: "Idealists devote much of their time to pursuing their own identity, their personal meaning, what they might signify -- their true Self.... The Self is a special part of the person -- a kind of personal essence or core of being, the vital seed of their nature.... NFs are passionate about finding this true Self, about becoming who they are, or self-actualized.... Idealists often dedicate their lives to this kind of self-realization -- seeking to become realized, trying to get in touch with the person they were meant to be, and to have an identity which is truly theirs.… The way to the Idealists' heart is to show them that we know their inner person, the Being behind the social role that must be played, behind the public mask (that) must be worn.… Because Idealists believe that each of us is a unique and special person, it makes sense that they would feel prized by having their person known by another, if only on rare occasions." (Keirsey 143-145)

After reading this description of NFs, we can see that the INFJ and INFPs certainly would be prone to Soul Misery. They may arrive at a state of despair if they cannot come to know who they are and understand why they are here. Simply put, for other personality types, answering these questions is just not as important.

ENFJs and ENFPs, although they are also Idealists in Keirsey's classification system, are less prone to Soul Misery because as extraverts they tend to be highly verbal and actively involved with their environment. Thus, they tend to have talked more freely about who they are and why they are here. They may have solicited many sources of information and taken many opportunities to talk and take action related to their feelings of

Soul Misery. They do not suffer alone, and they don't tend to feel all alone with their feelings. They feel seen, because they make sure they are -- by actively and frequently engaging with others. However, when an ENFJ or ENFP *does* suffer Soul Misery they do tend to isolate themselves, and are seen by those who know them well as acting out of character. Thus, their Soul Misery is recognized quickly by loved ones and they are encouraged to seek help. Soul Misery occurring in introverts may not be so easily identified because their behavior changes may not be as noticeable.

ISFPs tend to suffer Soul Misery because as a type, they do not tend to fit in with the pace of North American society. They are gentle, quiet, slow-paced individuals in a driven world. They tend to express themselves in quiet actions of caring for others, and love to spend hours just sitting and being with their friends and families. They are not ambitious people; yet, in our culture everyone must find a way to make a living. When ISFPs live with extraverted, ambitious parents who want their children to succeed in a material way, they feel miserable and out–of-step with their families -- families whom they love and want to make happy. In trying to please them, ISFPs fall out of line with the essence of who they are and why they are here. These individuals often seek life coaching because of their Soul Misery. Many say their misery stems from feeling like misfits in their careers. Keirsey recognized that ISFPs require some flexibility in their workplace. He recommended that ISFPs choose careers "that allow them a great deal of freedom and spontaneity. It is a sad day, indeed, when the ISFP chooses work wherein the operations are fixed by rule or ironclad necessity. To be happy and productive they must choose free, variable actions and be rewarded for doing them." (Keirsey 74)

Getting to know your personality type is a big step toward healing your Soul Misery, as you will then have a greater understanding of who you are. If you are able to see that you have been living out another personality type than your own, you will see more clearly why you have been feeling miserable. Your next task becomes bringing your life in line with your true personality type. This can take some time and effort, yet, each step you take in that direction will help you feel more and more yourself. Coming completely in line with the personality type you were born to be is a huge step in the direction of something I call deep personal congruence. We will explore this concept in the next section.

Personal Incongruence

When a person has no idea of who they are designed to be, they are in deep personal *incongruence*.

Soul Misery is healed when one comes into deep personal congruence. Deep personal congruence occurs when we discover and live in point-to-point alignment with who we are designed to be.

"Congruence" is not a word that is very familiar to us. Back in 1974, psychologist Carl Rogers first coined the term in relationship to the qualities of a psychotherapist.

"It has been found that personal change is facilitated when the psychotherapist is what he is, when in the relationship with the client he is genuine and without "front" or façade, openly *being* the feelings and attitudes which at that moment are flowing in him. We have coined the term "congruence" to try to describe this condition. By this we meant that the feelings the therapist is experiencing are available to him, available to his awareness and he is able to live these feelings, be them, and able to communicate them if appropriate" (qtd. in Brazier).

The American Heritage Dictionary of the English Language defines congruence as "agreement, harmony, conformity, or correspondence" (281).

Psychotherapist Dharmavidaya David Brazier explains it this way: "Loosely speaking, congruence means genuineness. People are congruent when they are not trying to appear as anything other than what they are. Congruence is the opposite of dissemblance. It is closely related to a number of other terms: authenticity, transparency, immediacy, spontaneity; yet its meaning does not precisely coincide with any of these." (Brazier. Amidatrust. 1993. March 29, 2011. www.amidatrust.com/ article congruence.html)

As we can see, congruence is difficult to define, yet when we are looking for it, we can experience it in relationship to another person. This person may be complimented for her "daring display of personal style". She may be called "the real deal". It may be said of her "what you see is what you get".

We are often able to pick out when what a person is saying and doing is not reflective of who they are inside. This is often the case when the person across from us is consciously putting on a show or a front.

At a deeper level, however, sometimes we do not pick up on incongruence, because the person across from us is not aware of being incongruent. They are living life to the best of their ability, as they have been socialized to live it, and they are unaware that who they are being is not who they were designed to be.

They may feel unhappy -- sometimes desperately unhappy -- with their life, but have no idea why. They may be married to a perfectly nice person, enjoy healthy, thriving children, own a lovely home, drive a good car and appreciate a well-paying job, but still they feel unhappy, and *for no good reason*, which makes the experience much worse.

This is the condition of deep personal incongruence. We may observe incongruence in others, but it is much more difficult to identify incongruence within ourselves when we are not consciously aware of our personality type, or when we have been knocked off that type through the process of domestication.

Deep personal incongruence also occurs when we lose contact with the very essence of ourselves.

I believe that each one of us was intentionally created by God in our mother's womb. I believe that we were each given specific physical characteristics, personality, gifts, talents and abilities that fit us for the unique purpose that God has in mind for us -- our original design. Of course, not everyone is comfortable with the word "God", and they may prefer to use another word, such as a Higher Power. When I express to a coaching client what I believe is true about there being an original design for us, on almost every occasion, regardless of their spiritual affiliation, each coaching client heaves a sigh of relief and says, "Yes, I have always felt that that is true." Being aware and believing in the concept of original design seems to bring a sense of hope and light and joy to each coaching client and to their unique situation. Because of domestication, we have a list of "shoulds" that control who we "should" be and what we "should" do. The thought that there is something deeper or higher for us to discover regarding who we are born to be -- and what we will love to do based on who we were created to be and do -- is a welcome one. In some ways, perhaps in our social relationships, it is easier to do what is expected of us, but we find real joy in knowing and following the path that appears when we become aware of our original design.

Likewise, when I examine a newborn baby, there is a sense of awe, and it feels like a holy moment every time, regardless of the parents' particular religious affiliation. We all feel the wonder and the mystery of a new life, as well as the responsibility to nurture that new and unique life. After examining so many newborns and watching them grow to maturity over twenty years of medical practice, I know it is possible to get a sense of the personality type of that newborn as early as the first few days after they are born. How wonderful if we trained ourselves as caregivers to look for and to nurture that unique person, rather than domesticating them the way we think we should, without regard for the uniqueness of each newborn child. Because of the tendency not to do this, it is entirely possible to reach adulthood having no idea that we have an original design, and therefore to live very far away from that master plan for our lives.

However, to live in line with our original design is to be in deep personal congruence. When we are in deep personal congruence, we feel contented, fulfilled and deeply satisfied within the core of ourselves, and although we can be affected by the external circumstances of our lives, within ourselves we feel settled and at peace.

Attaining deep personal congruence is a process that can take quite a while. However, with each new insight, you have the feeling that you are regaining an essential part of yourself. Each delicious discovery is another step toward healing Soul Misery. In subsequent chapters, we will see that there are four distinct stages a person passes through on this journey. In the next chapter I will describe each of these stages. In later chapters, we will talk about how you know you are in each stage and how you can progress through to the next. As you come into deep personal congruence in various areas of your life, you will go through the stages again and again, as many times as you need to, in order to feel that, at last, you have discovered all parts of yourself and you are allowing each part to be expressed in your life. Finding each of these parts and allowing its full expression is a lifelong adventure.

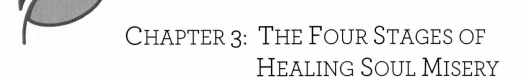

CHAPTER 3: THE FOUR STAGES OF HEALING SOUL MISERY

I believe that there are four stages we have to pass through in order to heal from Soul Misery.

These are:

I) *Awareness*

II) *Alignment*

III) *Authenticity*

IV) *Arrival*

The stage of *Awareness* is characterized by a blah, gray sensation of meaninglessness. You feel lost. This emptiness eventually intensifies into a feeling of deep and painful misery, which occurs when you can't separate your Self from the pain you are feeling about not being able to figure out *who you are* and *why you are here*. And, you cannot find any other person who sees who you are or why you are here. This creates a very painful feeling of loneliness, in addition to feeling lost.

It is only by fortunate serendipity that we find our way out of this stage. Something happens, or someone appears in our life who can give us a clue to the way out of this bleakness. Like the crocus that appeared in my mind's eye, or the article about the life coach in the newspaper, something must happen from outside ourselves to help us escape from the pain of *Awareness* and move into the next stage.

The second stage is *Alignment*. Here we find our way onto the path -- unique to us -- that will help us discover who we are and why we are on this planet. During this process of discovery we usually find fellow sojourners who can act as mirrors. These are people who can see us and reflect back to us who we are, as well as who we are in the process of becoming.

The third stage, *Authenticity,* is the stage during which we "go public" and begin to allow others to see what we are doing and who we are becoming. Often the people around us are upset by our changes. They want us to change back into the person we were previously. People can feel confused by our changes and feel unwilling or unable to accommodate them.

The fourth and final stage is *Arrival.* We finally know *who* we are and *why* we are, and others can see it, too. We feel content, calm, happy, and at peace as we come to understand what we need to be able to relax and enjoy our lives. Challenges will continue to come our way, but we can face them with equanimity because the core questions of our lives have been resolved. We have arrived!

I believe that we cycle through these four stages more than once on the way to healing our Soul Misery. Whenever we lose the feeling of fulfillment or we feel lost and alone, this signals that it is again time for us to grow in some substantial way. Growth and development will always be features of our lives. We may even come to embrace feeling out-of-sorts as an exciting sign that there is something new for us to discover about our lives or ourselves.

First Stage of Healing: Awareness

Awareness is the most difficult of the four stages of healing. There is so much pain associated with it. At first, you experience the gray numb feeling of meaninglessness. You have a sensation of not really belonging to this world -- of not fully engaging with it. Others seem to be having fun. They know who they are and what they are about, but you do not. You can put on a good show, and can seem fully involved in your life; in many ways you are because you probably hold down a job, are married and raising children. But underneath it all runs a current of needing something deeper and more meaningful than material success, a good job, a nice spouse and children. You feel ridiculous for feeling this way, especially as no one else around you seems to be experiencing the same yearning.

At a certain point, often during the mid-forties, this feeling of meaninglessness intensifies into deep misery. Despite your seeking, you are unable to find life's deeper meaning, and this becomes nearly impossible to bear. The feeling of being alone with your pain intensifies. You begin to feel deeply lost and the pain comes to dominate your life. It becomes urgent to find some answers. Who am I, *really?* Why am I here, *really?* Is there anyone else like me on this planet, someone who is struggling with the same issues that I am? You begin to feel that life is no longer worth living. Some people begin to think of driving their car into a tree, simply because carrying on in this manner seems too much to bear.

If you are reading this book, it is likely that you are in this stage of Awareness right now.

This is why something has to happen from outside your despair to change your situation. Sometimes it is God Himself who intervenes by way of a sign or an image. Sometimes a book comes to you, written by someone asking similar questions, and you don't feel as alone. Sometimes it is an encounter with someone who has been through similar pain, recognizes you as a fellow sufferer, and can give voice to what you haven't been able to speak about. This person is a mirror of your pain, and at the very least you no longer feel alone. This is what I believe the teaching coach did for me during that first crucial life coaching training weekend. She *saw* me. She looked at me with kind and compassionate eyes and asked questions that were meaningful and transformational for me. She helped me separate my Self from my pain; she gave me some objectivity about it and gave me a sense that there was a path forward. I thought if I continued training to be a life coach, I would receive more insights into how to heal both myself and my patients. I was able to replace the feeling of being lost and in despair with encouragement and hope.

God kindly provided me with the crocus image in my mind's eye to give me the first inkling of positive expectation. I still felt confused and deeply miserable, but I had a sense that something was about to change. In each of our lives, I believe there will come a moment when we are given a clue as to the pathway out of our pain. We don't know why we have to wait so long for that clue to appear, but at the right time, I believe it does. I am hopeful that this book will act as your "crocus" and act as a guide to finding the pathway out of Soul Misery.

When that pathway is shown you, and you decide to take it, the next stage -- the stage called *Alignment* -- can begin.

Second Stage of Healing: Alignment

Alignment is the process of coming into deep personal congruence. We become aware that there is an original design for each of us, and we are seeking to find it. In so doing, we answer two questions: *who am I?* and *why am I on this planet?* I want to describe for you what I do when I am working with a person who comes to me with Soul Misery. Of course, there is no one-size-fits-all approach, but I am going to describe the eight things that I offer to almost every coaching client, in the hope that they will come to know more clearly who they are and why they are here. As well, my hope is that each individual will feel "seen".

Personal Values

I begin the alignment process by helping my coaching client ascertain their personal values. Values are simply the things we value in life, the principles and ideas that are intrinsically desirable and important to our lives. A person's values are peculiar to that individual alone. I believe they are set into us while we are created in our mother's womb so as to fit us for the service God has in mind for us in this world. As a life coach, I have worked with hundreds of clients to help them identify their values and I have never seen any person with the same set of values as another. They are completely unique to that individual.

To ascertain values, I use a set of personal value cards. On a large table, I set out cards entitled: Must Have, High Want, Want, Indifferent, and Don't Want to function as column headings. The client holds the remaining seventy-five or so cards. Each one has a value written on it; the card could say, for example, *Freedom to Choose,* or *Honesty,* or *Peace.*

The instructions are: "Think about a deep, rich and satisfying life. In that life, where would each value belong? Must you have this value for your life to feel deep, rich and satisfying? Would it be a High Want? Would it be a Want? Would it be Indifferent? Would it be a Don't Want? Place the card in the column to which it belongs."

I sit and observe. In all cases, the client knows exactly where each value card belongs. When they have finished, I remove the cards they have placed under the headings Want, and Indifferent, as they are not of high enough importance to discuss further. It *is* important to me to find out why the client has placed values in the Must Have and High Want categories. It is equally important to discuss the values placed in the Don't Want category, as it is not possible for someone to feel happy and fulfilled if a Don't Want value is having to be adhered to in their life.

I then invite the client to define what each value means to them, as I know that people will define each one in their own way. I also ask them to tell me why each value would be necessary for their life to feel deep, rich and satisfying. In my experience, this is also easy for clients to determine. I think people actually know what they want in their lives, and they know how they have been designed; they simply have never been asked the questions that could draw out such information. At the end of the discussion, I read back notes I've taken as the client was speaking. This gives the person an overall report of what is required to have a life that feels rich, deep and satisfying *for them*. I ask the client to comment on any insights they gained about themselves while doing the exercise. I also ask permission to comment on what I have noticed while watching the person do the exercise. For example, I like to point out that I noticed how emphatically they placed a card such as *Freedom to Choose* under the Must Have column heading.

Overall, we come out of the Personal Value Card Exercise with important information to guide the ongoing personal growth of this individual. We have begun the process of discovering what values inform their life, and what makes them tick!

If you would like to try doing this exercise on your own at home, you can find the list of personal values that I use in Appendix II.

Personality Type

At our next meeting, I usually try to ascertain the client's Myers Briggs personality type. I use the method described in the book <u>Just My Type</u> by Paul Tieger and Barbara Barron-Tieger. This proves invaluable, as people have the experience of reading a description of their particular personality type. The client will usually laugh out loud and say, *"How can they know me that well?"*

For me, knowing that there are only sixteen personality types and that all the people I have coached have fit into one of these types -- and resonated with the description of their type -- gives further evidence of an original design plan at work. When a coaching client becomes aware of their personal values and their Myers

Briggs personality type, this information goes a long way toward answering the question *Who am I?*

Since almost all my Soul Misery clients are introverts, I then recommend they read Marti Laney's book, <u>The Introvert Advantage</u>. Her book describes the introvert personality in great detail, and identifies the benefits of being an introvert. Laney's book almost always has the effect on the introverted client of "coming home" to themselves. The client recognizes so many characteristics and aptitudes presented in the book -- characteristics and aptitudes they previously have not understood about themselves. There are far fewer introverts in our population than extroverts, so there are fewer "mirrors" in which introverts can recognize themselves or see themselves reflected. Laney's book, therefore, provides this positive and life-affirming experience.

Career Exploration

Many Soul Misery clients come to see me because they labor in careers that feel woefully unsatisfying. These clients have not yet been able to answer the question *Why am I here?* It naturally follows, then, for us to explore careers that would best suit their given nature and abilities.

I ask the client to pick up the Tiegers' book <u>Do What You Are</u> and study the chapter devoted to their personality type. In that chapter appears a list of ten elements that -- for this specific personality type -- would make for career satisfaction. Having the client read through that list *and agree with those elements* is a good double check that we have together identified their correct personality type.

From the listings of popular occupations for their type, I ask the client to indicate which are of interest to them. I often note, ruefully, that the client's current job is not among those best suited for their type.

For the time being, we set aside those possible future careers. Instead, we revisit the subject of the client's values, this time in relation to their work life. We play a version of the Personal Values Exercise, this time using value cards that pertain to career. The client can select values such as *Friendships at Work* or *Alignment with the Boss* or *Artistic Creativity.* In the same way, we discuss what each value word means for them, and why they chose it. At the end, in order to give an overall view of what the client has said,

I read back the values they have chosen and what they said about each. And, once more, I notice that people never have a problem identifying their Must Have, High Want and Don't Want values as they regard careers.

Together -- based on the client's Myers Briggs personality type and their career values -- we determine which careers would provide pleasure and satisfaction, rather than the alienation and purposelessness they may currently experience.

At this stage, the client has a much clearer idea of what they are suited to do and why they may be here in this world. For instance, a classroom teacher discovered she was much more suited for a career as a social worker. This explained why she did not like to prepare lesson plans very much, but that she loved speaking one-on-one with her students.

For some, the career exploration work heralds a moment of profound insight. I have seen clients go out, quit their job that very day, and enroll as soon as possible in a program to prepare them for a career they are infinitely more suited to -- an occupation they were born to do. And they do this with such gladness and certainty! It is a step towards deep personal congruence for the Soul Misery sufferer. Doing satisfying work that is in line with your values, your gifts, talents and abilities can ease the pain of feeling like a misfit, even though you may have been a highly respected professional. It really doesn't matter, if that profession does not feel like it is the right one for you.

Art Making

I often use art very early on in meeting with a client who is suffering Soul Misery.

For instance, I will ask them to make me two sketches, one entitled "The Way It Is" and a second called "The Way I Want It To Be". Looking at what the client has drawn and then discussing the piece, often gives us useful information about where the client is right now: how distressed they are about their Soul Misery and why they are distressed -- what exactly is going on. This simple art-making technique can quickly and easily clarify how they feel, because it bypasses the left / thinking part of their brain. The right / intuitive brain holds so much valuable information and we need to access that information.

Many clients claim they can't draw. So many people have been criticized during art classes in school. But when I give them permission to make an abstract drawing, this usually liberates them to draw a free, childlike representation of how they truly feel. Since "How I Want It To Be" is a representation of their hopes and dreams, it provides some enjoyable discussion.

One client made a series of five paintings within a few minutes that represented how she would progress from the way it is to the way she wanted it to be. She used dollar-store fluid acrylic paints and worked from the squeeze bottles directly onto the paper.

They were entitled:

1) Ignoring My Heart
2) Picking up the Pieces
3) Hopefully, Adding Color
4) But to feel Safe, I need Structure
5) But what I really want is to feel free, unfettered, being free to be all of me.

Interestingly, although this client did weep while making her paintings, and we did have an emotional, fruitful discussion of what these paintings meant to her, she didn't want to see them again after that session. Some clients, however, keep their sketches and use them to assess their progress. Sometimes I keep them in my chart and we refer back to them as, together, we heal their Soul Misery.

Assessment of Depression

Over eight years of coaching clients with Soul Misery, I have learned to assess fairly early in the process whether they are clinically depressed. Roughly fifty percent of clients are depressed at their first presentation to me. They have suffered so long with their Soul Misery that it has slipped into a clinical depression. I use two main assessment tools to ascertain this diagnosis: the mnemonic tool called SIGECAPS and the Beck Depression Inventory. The SIGECAPS test can easily be found and scored online, for any of you who would like to see it. Of course, it is best to get the assessment of a family physician or psychiatrist, as well.

If a patient /client is depressed, I find the best thing to do in most instances is to treat the depression before proceeding with the coaching. Without treatment, the work goes much more slowly, and sometimes starts going in circles. At times, it is difficult to see that the person is actually depressed, granted, but when progress is slow and laden with guilt and self-doubt, this is my clue to ask the patient to take one of the depression inventories. We then think seriously together about whether they may be suffering from a clinical depression in addition to Soul Misery. When the patient/client is feeling somewhat better, usually within six to eight weeks, we can proceed; the person is on more solid footing to be able to do the work required for healing their Soul Misery.

The Bigger Game

In December 2009, I discovered the Bigger Game workshop. This workshop is designed to answer the questions: *what is my compelling purpose?* and *what is a practical way I could live this out on the planet?*

To understand your compelling purpose is to access deep self-knowledge. *Why am I doing what I am doing? What am I truly about?* With these questions answered, we become clear about the kind of "bigger game" we wish to create. Throughout our lives, we are always playing a game, i.e. we are always contributing in some way to the world and ourselves. A Bigger Game is something bigger than us, and cannot be played on our own. We need allies, people to help us succeed in achieving our goals. For instance, I came to see that my compelling purpose is to help others see clearly for the sake of their personal freedom. A way I could live this out was to write this book. Writing and publishing a book requires editors, graphic designers, proofreaders, marketers, and many friends and family cheering one on; it definitely cannot be achieved by oneself. This is what makes it a bigger game.

Understanding our compelling purpose enables us to rise to a goal that compels us deeply on a personal level *and* impacts the world around us. When we tap into our compelling purpose -- when we are up to something bigger than simply surviving -- it feels deeply satisfying and fulfilling. When we are compelled and doing something with all our might for very good reasons we can achieve amazing things.

Attending a Bigger Game workshop is something I offer coaching clients after offering them the other tools I've discussed. I think they get the most value from the workshop after working on their own and one-and-one with me to heal their Soul Misery. Because the Bigger Game is a group event involving a series of exercises, a participant must be feeling well enough to be able to engage in the group process. They must have made enough progress in their own healing to be equally interested in helping other group members discover their compelling purpose and bigger game.

My experience is that all the clients who attend the workshop find it useful in their quest to answer profound questions about their personal and professional lives. The exercises are generic enough to appeal to all personality types, but INFJ and INFP personality types especially enjoy the chance to look intensely at the deep meaning of their lives.

The Bigger Game workshop is structured around a game board that becomes a template for self-coaching. It teaches participants how to keep new insights alive, and it provides a way to continue developing the ideas for one's own bigger game.

A lovely by-product of the workshop is that participants often meet other seekers with like or similar personality types. The experience fosters many friendships and alliances. It is a sweet experience to meet others who see you -- who *get* you – and, who like you, have a keen interest in achieving goals in the world. You can learn more about this workshop by viewing the website www.biggergame.com.

Recovering Lost Parts of Ourselves

Because of the work you have done discovering your personal values, learning about your personality type, and thinking about what your compelling purpose might be, you begin to exercise whole new parts of your brain that you may not have accessed for some time. You become open to new ideas. You are willing to notice and acknowledge hidden parts of yourself -- elements that were not encouraged to flourish during your domestication process. It's not that you were unwilling to see these parts in the past, as much as you were not encouraged to see them.

In my own case, I had no idea that I could be an artist. I had a negative experience about making art in elementary school when a teacher found my creations to be wanting, and said so in front of my class. I decided I would never make art again. Yet, when I began seeing images in my mind's eye and asked for help to make them, I realized that I *am* an artist -- in fact, an artist with a backlog of pieces to make! It was through the kindness of my artist friend, and her patience, encouragement and willingness to see me as an artist that this creative part of me received the conditions to emerge.

I have found that my Soul Misery clients have similar experiences. They remember -- or discover for the first time -- a love for art making, dance, music or writing. This brings so much joy to their lives. Art, too, acts as a vehicle for further self-discovery, and sharing those discoveries. Many of my Soul Misery clients have found they enjoy dance as much as I do, and many of them have found pleasure in writing poetry. Some discovered they are artists, as I did, and have gone on to make and show their art.

A patient of mine, Shannon Moroney, discovered that she was an acrylic abstract artist. She has gone on to write a book about her experiences, and many of her own paintings are included. She also gives talks about the importance of art making in healing. Her website is www.shannonmoroney.com, if you are interested in reading further about her journey.

My own passion for dance was awakened during some instruction I was taking in the use of expressive arts in healing. One morning we were introduced to a dance form called Nia, a form of exercise that incorporates movements from each of three martial arts, three dance arts, and three healing arts. As our teacher, Martha Randall led us through a sixty-minute Nia routine, I cried the whole way through. I recognized this was a type of exercise I would enjoy for the rest of my life.

Likewise, you may discover expressive arts that feel meaningful to you. What is required on your part is a curious, exploring spirit, and a willingness to try new things -- a small price to pay for the sake of finding those special activities that resonate with you deeply -- activities just right for you.

Finding the Powerful Perspective

During the course of healing Soul Misery sufferers, I introduce them to the concept of perspective. I teach them how to choose the most powerful perspective possible in each situation they face. I learned this principle during coaching training. In each circumstance we come upon, we view that circumstance from a certain viewpoint. Depending on the viewpoint, it will either serve us or hinder us in handling that particular situation. Simply put, we must consciously seek the most powerful, useful, helpful perspective to be able to experience our lives with equanimity, self-control, ease and a feeling of personal choice and power. This is an important skill for a Soul Misery sufferer to acquire.

At a certain point, each Soul Misery sufferer comes to the place where they are ready to start putting some of the things they have learned about themselves and their lives into practice. When that day comes, they enter the stage called *Authenticity.*

THIRD STAGE OF HEALING: AUTHENTICITY

In the previous two stages of healing Soul Misery, *Awareness* and *Alignment,* the people around you may not be aware that things have changed regarding the way you are choosing to live your life. For example, you are now living much more intentionally because you know what your personal values are, and you are trying to live highly in them. You know about the concept of trying to live from the most powerful perspective you can find, and you are attempting to do that. In other words, you are trying to live your life according to your own values, rather than the values of your parents or society.

Your Soul Misery was a hidden misery, and so far, your process of coming into alignment with your original design has been hidden also. The growth you have undertaken is often a solitary and personal pursuit. It is as if new, deep root systems have developed within you that no one else can see. You feel safe and protected as you grow like a plant in a greenhouse or in a sheltered corner of the garden. Your fresh ideas and new ways may not have been exposed to friends, family and colleagues. They have yet to be tested in your outer world.

During *Authenticity,* you begin to let others see what you are up to and who you are becoming. People may be upset by your changes, and they may actually be unwilling to see you in the new way that you see yourself. They would rather you revert to behaving like the person they were familiar with and comfortable being around. Your changes can confuse people and they may be unwilling to accommodate to them.

However, in the process of healing your Soul Misery there comes a time when there is nothing else you can do; you are compelled to go against aspects of the domestication process of your childhood. Change must happen. A new day is coming and nothing else will suffice. This is the stage of taking a stand for yourself, for your right to be who you are and who you are becoming. You have a right to continue making changes that you discover are in line with who you are and why you are here. And as some people resist the "new you", you feel a good bit of annoyance at their unwillingness to accept what you are experiencing as personal growth.

The process of taking a stand for yourself can be difficult, to say the least. It is a process that can feel raw, new, sacred, exciting and fearful all at once. It takes courage to do the work to discover what is true for you, but acting upon this truth can be even more challenging. You are trying to actualize what you know theoretically. You do it for the sake of continuing to feel that you are coming into alignment with the individual God made you to be in the world. You do it so you can stay alive, and feel fully alive as you walk your path. It is not enough to simply know who you are and why you are here. Taking steps to act on your newfound knowledge makes what you have learned more real for you, both in your internal world, and in the world around you. Just having "head" knowledge does not satisfy. The outworking of what you know produces fruit, and when you are acting upon what you know, you learn yet more about yourself, which prompts other new actions.

This process of knowing and then actualizing is accomplished in stages. In fact, it is easier to know a truth and then act upon it, and then know the next truth and act upon *it*, rather than absorbing all the knowledge and trying to implement everything at once. When you are trying to make changes in your external life, a tipping point is reached. You must take a step away from what is currently safe, comfortable and known. "The known" leads to approval and security. Stepping into the unknown implies that change will occur in how people see you, and even more profoundly, there will be a change in how you see yourself. The process of balancing on the tipping point, the moment before taking the leap into the unknown, can produce a feeling of crazy chaos within your head. You are neither this, nor that, and you may feel as if you are swaying back and forth between the safe, secure known and the exciting, somewhat-fearful unknown. At times like this, you need to anchor yourself to people who are either moving in the same direction of personal growth as you, or to people who are rock-solid and stable in their lives.

It is as though there is a mountain ahead of you. You are standing at the base of the mountain on one side, looking to ascend the mountain and then slide down the other side into living over there in that new place. You have a rope around your waist, and this rope goes up and over the mountain. It is attached to your supporters -- fellow sojourners on the path to the fulfilled life, as well as to rock-solid settled friends who have made the journey ahead of you. The moment comes when you are prepared to take the journey up and over the mountain, to live on that other side.

You must make the decision to take that journey, yet you can secure yourself to your allies and supporters and make your move!

Once you begin taking definite action in this way, William Hutchinson Murray's piece about commitment may transform from words on a page to a series of events in your own experience.

Commitment

Until one is committed there is hesitation –
the chance to draw back -- always ineffectiveness.
Concerning all acts of initiative and creation there is one
elementary truth; the moment one definitely commits oneself,
Providence moves, too.
All sorts of things occur to help one that would never otherwise
have occurred.
A whole stream of events issue from the decision rising in one's
favor.
All manner of unforeseen incidents and meeting and material
assistance, which no man could have dreamed would have come
his way. (Murray, William. March 31st, 2011. http://www.thinkexist.com/quotation/ until one is committed)

This occurred in my own life when I made the decision to inquire about buying a building with the perfect proportions to create an art studio and an expressive arts therapy space. It turned out the building *was* available and I was able to buy it as part of an ownership group, which lessened the financial risk for me. I was able to find the perfect contractor to help me transform the space into an art studio, and at an affordable price. All sorts of details fell into place to make my dream come true that I could never have anticipated. Over the past three years of working out of the studio, I have been able to host art shows, hold Nia dance classes, open the space to community groups for their use, use it to conduct life coaching with my own clients, as well as to make art and relax in the space myself.

The *Authenticity* stage contains elements of the "hero's journey" that the mythologist Joseph Campbell wrote about. In fables and myths throughout the world, Campbell identified a pattern: the hero must venture outside the realm he knows if he is to win love, save his community or right a wrong. In order to actualize our dreams, we, too, must take risks, step outside our known world and do something different than we have done in the past.

A truism is that when you take action for the right reasons, what you do and who you subsequently become, ends up serving not just yourself, but the world. Few maxims are more thrilling to experience.

I have found the recipe for successful change is the following:

Enough misery + enough clarity + enough cups of love and encouragement poured upon us + enough courage = successful change

It seems we need each of these elements to make the changes that bring our beliefs and our actions into alignment with what we come to know is true for ourselves. In my experience, this is good for us -- good for the health of our individual minds, bodies, emotions and spirits. We become open to deep contentment and joy.

In my own life, my domestication as a woman, a physician and a Christian, dictated that I must always put others' needs before my own. I was to serve selflessly, never saying no to any reasonable request made of me. But when I decided to transfer two hundred of my regular family practice patients to a new young family physician in my town, I did it purely for my own benefit. I wanted to make room in my days to increase the amount of life coaching I did, and to have time to travel and present Bigger Game workshops. When I began to do life coaching, I started to create two parallel worlds of service in my life. One was a world where I continued to care for my nine hundred patients. The other was a world where I made art, wrote books, led Nia classes, facilitated Bigger Game workshops and conducted life coaching. I managed both of these worlds until the day came when it felt impossible to continue this way. I had reached "gridlock". I had no room to sign-on new family practice patients, or to accept more life-coaching clients, or to explore interesting workshop opportunities. Change *had* to happen, and it had to happen *now.*

A series of circumstances occurred to help me realize that the time had arrived. It will happen for you, too. When you know you want to make a change, you must learn to watch for the signs. I learned not to force change, but rather wait for the right time. For example, I had wanted to decrease the size of my family practice for two years before I actually made the decision to do so. I had wanted to wait for another family physician to come along who I thought would do a really good job of caring for my patients -- someone who had a similar philosophy of how to practice family medicine. Just when I thought I couldn't wait any longer, the right physician appeared. He was a new graduate, willing to take on some of my practice.

Joyfully, I wrote a letter to my patients explaining my plans and the changes that were about to occur. Even though I had found a wonderful replacement physician, I was not prepared for how difficult it would be to actually make the change. As I experienced some bodily symptoms, headache and stomach upset, I discovered that after thirty years of being a family physician, changing my pattern of serving people proved more difficult than I had anticipated.

In the end, thinking, waiting and praying -- plus the conviction that I was doing the right thing for me -- won over my emotions and my bodily reactions to change. I had come to see that personal fulfillment, contentment and a sense of alignment with God's purposes for me came from conducting my life in accordance with my values, my compelling purpose and from what I understood to be my gifts. This contentment also arose from listening to what I believed God was calling me to do at that moment.

When you make your decisions and changes in this way and for these reasons, you will progress to the stage of *Arrival*, which is characterized by contentment as deep and calm and peaceful as the ocean on a perfect day.

FOURTH STAGE OF HEALING: ARRIVAL

The stage of *Arrival* is characterized by the lovely experience of feeling calm and contented, unrushed and relaxed. On many occasions, shots of joy course through you. You feel, finally, that you know who you are and why you are here, and you get to act from that centered, certain, uncluttered place. You have friends who see you, who *get* you -- and you see and *get* them. You have regular contact with these people, and life feels rich, deep and satisfying.

In this stage, people no longer try to persuade you to see things their way, or live in ways that suit them. Rather, people notice your peace and joy and start to ask how you attained them. Blessedly, you have consciously chosen your path and you are walking upon it. You no longer seek wildly for insight because you have found the key to enjoying life:

Authenticity + Clarity + Courage = Simplicity + Peace + Freedom.

By going through many cycles of *Awareness, Alignment, Authenticity and Arrival,* you have discovered what matters to you and who matters to you. You are at peace with the array of gifts, talents and abilities you have been given because you see how they can be used to bring joy to yourself as you serve others in this world. In this place of ease and flow, life feels increasingly simple and uncomplicated. Writer/broadcaster and former Bishop of the Scottish Episcopal Church in Edinburgh, Richard Holloway, put it this way:

"*Simplicity, clarity, singleness. These are the attributes that give our lives power and vividness and joy, as they are also the marks of great art. They seem to be the purpose of God for His whole creation.*" (Holloway, Richard. March 31st, 2011. http://thinkexist.com/quotation/ simplicity-clarity-singleness)

You see that we human beings are each one piece of the jigsaw puzzle that is humanity. You are at peace with being the piece you are, and you see, respect and enjoy other human beings as they contribute their unique piece to the puzzle.

Once you experience the state of *Arrival* and know deep inside how it feels, you will want to return to this state should you become knocked off-center. You will be willing to do what it takes to regain your equilibrium, even displeasing or disappointing others, while at the same time respecting them and their needs. When you feel contentment you know that you have found your proper place of service -- a place that gives you joy. There may well be challenges to overcome as you serve, but you undertake them gladly because they, too, are part of your path.

Arrival is the experience of deep personal congruence. You feel that you are living in point-to-point alignment with who you were born to be. Your body is also at peace. You no longer experience stomach upset, twitching eyelids, palpitations or frequent headaches. Our bodies act as amazing navigators; they clearly tell us when we are on the right track.

When you think about your personal values, you realize that you are living highly in *all* of them, not just some of them. You come from the powerful perspective of knowing who you are and why you are choosing to serve in the ways that you do. You have thought about your compelling purpose statement -- discovered during the Bigger Game workshop, or during personal life coaching -- and have figured out your way to live it in the world. This is the compass you use to make sure you are on-course in your life; it guides your decisions about how to spend your life's energy.

You are at peace with the people in your life because you are sending out calm, happy signals to others. And they will tend to respond in kind.

The stage of *Arrival* is your reward for all the hard work you have done up to now. You have sought illumination, direction, your identity and your purpose for being here "*as a man whose hair is on fire seeks a pond*". Your newfound knowledge is your prize and your treasure. Enjoy it! Think back on the journey you have taken to arrive at this place. Although you may yet again go through the cycle of Awareness, Alignment, Authenticity and Arrival, take time to give thanks for where you are today in your journey. Give thanks for your guides along the way: the people, the workshops, the books, your God. You have arrived!

Appendix I: Booklist for the Journey

Barron-Tieger, Barbara and Tieger, Paul. *Do What You Are*. New York: Little Brown Publishing, 1992.

This book helps us identify what jobs are ideal for our unique personality type using Myers Briggs personality typing.

Barron-Tieger, Barbara and Tieger, Paul. *Just Your Type*. New York: Little Brown Publishing, 2002.

This book explains how relationships work between all possible combinations of personality types. It explains both the joys and the frustrations of each personality pairing, and gives helpful advice for how each personality pairing can best function together.

Cameron, Julia. *Finding Water: The Art of Perseverance.* New York: Penguin Books, 2006.

> This book is a huge help in understanding the encouragement that INFJ/INFP personality types need to do their work in the world. The beautiful concept of Believing Mirrors is found in this book.

Campbell, Joseph. *Reflections on the Art of Living: A Joseph Campbell Companion* selected and edited by Diane K. Osbon. New York: Harper Perennial, 1991.

> This book is a collection of Joseph Campbell's wise and insightful quotations as well as his thoughts about life's main themes. This one really got me thinking about what is truly important in life and what is "just details".

Chapman, Gary. *The Five Love Languages.* Chicago: Northfield Publishing, 1992.

> This books tells us that there are five different ways to express love in a relationship, and helps us discover which way is our way, and then how we can best relate to people who give and receive love in a different language than we do.

Goldberg, Natalie. *Writing Down the Bones*. Boston: Shambhala Publications, 2005.

This book is so kind, helpful, firm and insightful about what it takes to become a writer. It's simple, yet elegant and thorough.

Hollis, James. *Finding Meaning in the Second Half of Life: How to Finally, Really Grow up*. New York: Gotham Books, 2005.

I think Chapter 5: The Dynamics of Intimate Relationships is a must-read for all of us. We tend to think that if we could just find that "magical other", all our misery would go away. Not so! It is our responsibility to meet our own deepest needs.

Hollis, James. *Why Good People Do Bad Things: Understanding Our Darker Selves*. New York: Gotham Books, 2007.

This book is an amazing exposition of the Shadow that we all have, the complexes and imagoes that can run our lives when we are unconscious of them. To read and to understand and to incorporate what he says into our lives, is to take some big steps forward on our journey to freedom.

Hollis, James. *What Matters Most: Living A More Considered Life.* New York: Gotham Books, 2009.

> This book introduces us in a very understandable way to practical, useful, applicable Jungian psychoanalytical concepts regarding things that can hold us back in our personal lives. He exhorts us not to allow fear or lethargy hold us back from attaining what matters most in life.

Keirsey, David. *Please Understand Me II: Temperament, Character, Intelligence. New York:* Prometheus Nemesis Book Company, 1998.

> This book explains the concept of temperament, and helps us understand why certain personality types may be more prone to soul misery than others.

Laney, Marti. *The Introvert Advantage.* New York: Workman Publishing, 2002.

> This is the first book I have read that explains clearly what is good about being an introvert. Very good reframing!

MacLeod, Hugh. *Ignore Everybody and 39 Other Keys to Creativity.* New York: Portfolio Publishing, 2009.

> This is a book that helps you develop the insight and courage to be and do what you are, boldly and without apology!

Moore, Thomas. *Soul Mates: Honoring the Mysteries of Love and Relationship.* New York: Harper Perennial, 1994.

> Soul Misery sufferers really need soul mates! This book introduces us to the concept of what a "soul mate" is: people who understand us deeply and who will agree to walk life's journey side-by-side with us.

Moore, Thomas. *Original Self.* New York: Harper Collins, 2000.

> The idea of original design is not a new one. Thomas Moore explains the concept beautifully in his series of short essays about what he terms the "original self". Inspiring!

Mountain Dreamer, Oriah. *The Call.* New York: Harper Collins, 2003.

Mountain Dreamer, Oriah. *The Invitation.* New York: Harper Collins, 1999.

These books speak to the concept of deep personal congruence. They are books to savor and enjoy!

O'Donohue, John. *Anam Cara: A Book of Celtic Wisdom.* New York: Harper Perennial, 1997.

Soul Misery sufferers need food for their souls. John O'Donohue is a master of this! John espouses the idea that there is a unique design for each individual, and he encourages us to discover it and live it.

O'Donohue, John. *Beauty: The Invisible Embrace.* New York: Harper Collins, 2004.

This book is more beautiful food for our soul, inspiring and encouraging us to look for the beauty in life all around us.

Ruiz, Don Miguel. *The Four Agreements*. San Rafael: Amber Allen Publishing, 1997.

> This book makes it clear how we forget who we are born to be, and gives us help for healing the wounds of "domestication".

Ruiz, Don Miguel. *The Mastery of Love*. San Rafael: Amber Allen Publishing, 1999.

> This book explains how and why we wound each other and how we can learn to become nonjudgmental and helpful to others on our journey.

Whitworth, Laura, Tamlyn, Rick and MacNeill Hall, Caroline. *The Bigger Game*. Outskirts Press, 2009.

> The book The Bigger Game, explains in more detail the concepts that are presented in the Bigger Game two-day workshop. After attending this program, I became much clearer about my compelling purpose.

Appendix II: Personal Values

Ability to influence	Achievement	Advancement
Adventure	Affection	Authenticity
Beauty	Challenge	Change and Variety
Comfort	Community	Companionship
Competition	Communication	Conformity
Connection	Contentment	Contribution
Control	Cooperation	Courage
Creativity	Directness	Economic Security
Elegance	Endurance	Expertness
Fairness	Family	Flexibility
Freedom	Friendship	Generosity
Gentleness	Good Health	Happiness
Helpfulness	Honesty	Hopefulness
Humor	Independence	Inner Harmony
Integrity	Involvement	Knowledge
Leadership	Love	Loyalty
Mercy	Mortality and Ethics	Order
Passion	Peace	Philanthropy
Physical Challenge	Personal Development	Play
Power	Predictability	Recognition
Relaxation	Religious Belief	Responsibility
Risk	Security	Self-Respect
Spirituality	Stability	Strength
Tradition	Travel	Trust
Uniqueness	Wealth	Wisdom

 # BIBLIOGRAPHY

Barron Tieger, Barbara and Tieger, Paul. *Do What You Are*. New York: Little Brown Publishing, 1992.

Barron Tieger, Barbara and Tieger, Paul. *Just Your Type*. New York: Little Brown Publishing, 2002.

Bigger Game Workshop http://www.biggergame.com.

Brazier, David. "Congruence". 1993. http://amidatrust.com.

Campbell, Joseph. *Reflections on the Art of Living: A Joseph Campbell Companion* selected and edited by Diane K. Osbon. New York: Harper Perennial, 1991.

Holloway, Richard. http://thinkexist.com.

Keirsey, David. *Please Understand Me II: Temperament, Character, Intelligence. New York:* Prometheus Nemesis Book Company, 1998.

Laney, Marti. *The Introvert Advantage*. New York: Workman Publishing, 2002.

Moroney, Shannon. http://shannonmoroney.com.

Murray, William Hutchinson. http://www.thinkexist.com.

Ruiz, Don Miguel. *The Four Agreements*. San Rafael: Amber Allen Publishing, 1997.

Ruiz, Don Miguel. *The Mastery of Love*. San Rafael: Amber Allen Publishing, 1999.

Whitworth, Laura, Tamlyn, Rick and MacNeill Hall, Caroline. *The Bigger Game*. Outskirts Press, 2009.

 ABOUT THE AUTHOR

Susan Gleeson has practiced family medicine for over thirty years. Wanting to deepen her ability to heal, she became a certified life coach through the Coaches Training Institute in 2004. The following year she completed the Organization and Relationship Systems Coaching Program of the Coaches Training Institute. Susan then began to learn about using expressive arts in healing, and is taking courses towards the Expressive Arts Certificate offered at the Haliburton School of the Arts in Ontario, Canada. Susan is a certified Nia teacher, and has attained her Blue Belt in this cardiovascular program that incorporates music and expressive movement. Susan has also completed the Coaches Training Institute Co-active Leadership program and experienced the Bigger Game workshop led by Rick Tamlyn. In 2010, she became a certified Bigger Game trainer.

Susan is devoted to helping people see the truth about their lives for the sake of their personal freedom and health. It is Susan's dearest hope that this book has helped the reader on their own journey towards clarity, freedom and good health.